&

REALITY

‒‒‒∞‒‒‒

BK Jayanti

A BK Publications Book

First Publication 2000
Second Publication 2010

ISBN 978-1-886872-19-6

Published by the Brahma Kumaris Information Services,
Ltd. Global Co-operation House, 65 Pound Lane, London
NW10 2HH, UK

Designed by Sameer Patro
Printed in India by Imprint Digital Ltd.

Contents

MIND MAPS

For most people today, more information than ever before is available about the world around us. Nevertheless, we often grow up with only a limited understanding and awareness of the world inside us – our thoughts, feelings, attitudes and emotions. Even when we do take closer look at some of these internal goings-on, we tend to feel that they are largely dictated by external events. However that need not be so. Improved

knowledge of the deeper self
and the inner landscape
over which the mind ranges,
can immeasurably improve
the quality of life's journey,
providing orientation,
widening horizons and
opening up new directions.
Mind Maps is a series of short
spiritual guides to help the
traveller along the way.

A
Spiritual
Model

What are dreams and what is reality? To approach this topic I would first like to share with you a simple model of the eternal soul. The soul is one of two aspects of the human being. There is the body, which is physical, and therefore temporary. Quite distinct from the body, there is the soul, which is not physical, but metaphysical and spiritual. I would describe the soul as a point of light which is located behind the middle of the forehead.

A model of this point of light, the soul, will provide us with the map we need to lead us into deeper understanding of the topic of dreams and reality. This map of the soul has been well charted by different mystics and yogis through their experiences and is open to exploration by anyone.

The dynamic of the human experience is the interplay of energies between the soul and the body. The energy which the soul generates reaches the brain and from there the energy reaches the rest of the body.

How does the mind fit into this model? Is it part of the body – just an epiphenomenon of the brain – or part of the soul? I would suggest that the mind is actually a function within the anatomy of the soul: a spiritual organ or capability of the soul.

The
Conscious
And
Subconcious
Mind

Looking inside and seeing what is happening within 'I', the being of light, the soul, the first thing we discover as we journey inwards is our ability to think – the mind. The mind generates thoughts. At this level of the soul, we can observe our thoughts in a very conscious way. I am aware of those thoughts and, if I choose, I can be the master of those thoughts and direct them purposefully. Deeper than the conscious mind is an area of the soul, the second area, which includes the vast subconscious. So our model of the soul includes the notion that the soul is deep and has various layers or levels. Amongst these layers of the soul is a place that contains all the experiences that I have accumulated in the past, i.e. a place within which I carry the imprint or recording of all the experiences that I have ever had.

A stimulus that reaches me from outside, through my eyes, ears, or other sense organs, will touch this place within and trigger thoughts in response to that stimulus. Our multi-layered model then also becomes cyclical: thoughts and actions make their imprint and on the basis of that imprint, further thoughts arise.

What is Reality?

With this in mind, what does 'reality' mean? We often think of reality in physical terms, using the senses of the body and they do indeed tell us a lot. But if in this materialistic world we allow our approach to materialistic we will ignore the spiritual dimension of life and so forget that reality includes more than just this material world. Just as the whole person comprises body and soul, reality is the combination of the spiritual and physical dimensions. It is this that is the totality of life. We cannot mechanically quantify and label everything that happens to us. Look, for example, at an experience as simple as eating. It seems simple enough, and it is something that happens many times during the space of each day and so is familiar to us but is actually quite complex. When I eat something, is the sum total of my experience X% of carbohydrate and protein, and so on? Definitely not! So what is it? Even if you and I eat the same bread,

for me it may be delicious,
for you perhaps it is not. My
point is that there are many
intangible and variable
factors in every act we
perform.

When I have an experience,
even though it may be coming
to me from the physical
senses, it is not just a physical
sensation. The experience of
eating is not just what my
taste buds are telling me, but
it also includes memories.
I eat a particular dish or
item of food and it reminds

me of other situations and experiences. So if the experience of eating is so complex, how much more complex is the experience of meeting and relating to another human being – how many intangibles are involved within.

Reality, therefore, is not just what I can touch and feel, but is a vast experience, much more than the sum total of the information that comes from my physical senses.

My perception only shows me little parts of reality within time and space. Maybe there can come a point when there is such a development of consciousness that I am able to know more and more of reality until I can glimpse that which has been described as Truth. To do this, I must not restrict myself to an awareness – often over-emphasised – of the body and its senses, which bring me information. Instead, I must begin to focus on the inner self that processes that information and knows and experiences reality. I must distinguish knowledge from the self that knows.

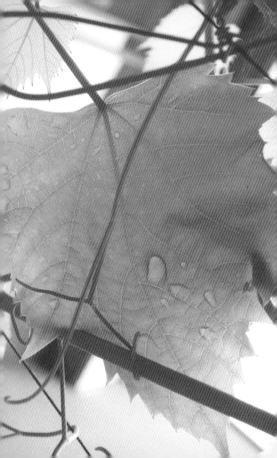

Dreams

So much for reality; what about the other side – the dream? We often think of dreams as being the opposite of reality, but in fact there is not such a big difference between dreams and reality. To gain a clearer understanding of dreams let us first look at what happens during that period described as sleep.

Sleep is a time when the body's need for rest is met, a time when my own inner being is also at rest. At this

point another factor within
the model of the soul needs to
be mentioned. It is the third
aspect or organ of the soul
and it completes the model.
This aspect of the soul is
called the intellect.

The intellect is the conscious
ability to discern, to decide,
and to judge. It is the filter
between thought and action.
At the time when the body
is resting, the soul is also
taking opportunity to rest,
but although the intellect
remains inactive throughout

the period of sleep, the mind does not rest. This is how the experiences we have had during the day can be processed whilst we sleep.

Every human being dreams, whether we remember our dreams or not. When there is disruption within the sleep cycle and we are not allowed to dream then it is found that, on waking, we can get disoriented within a very short space of time. On the basis of the above spiritual model and from observing my own experience, I have come to understand that what happens during the time of sleep is a result of what has happened within me during the day.

Waking Experience and Dreams

The experience we often have during the day is rush, rush with no time to look within, no time to reflect. It is during the period of sleep that I go through the events of the day, and the subconscious and unconscious reactions of the day, without their going through the conscious filter of the intellect. Because of this, dreams tend to come out jumbled. Different experiences that have happened in a sequence in time become disjointed and perhaps not completely understandable

and yet there is a signal, a
deep logic, a message that is
there for me to understand.

What is happening is
that the experiences and
images recorded within the
subconscious part of the soul
are coming up onto the screen
of my mind, and through
this process the imprint,
or recording within the
subconscious becomes even
more firmly fixed.

So some memory of the past,
for example, images of people

I met perhaps many years ago and have forgotten, might come up in some form or another and when they do so, they give me signals. Maybe they tell me of a deep unresolved relationship of dependence that I was not aware of or had not dealt with. The following story is a simple example told to me by someone actively committed to bringing spirituality into their life.

This person had been in a situation in which a little

earlier in their life they would have reacted with anger. However, their spiritual endeavour was such that they suppressed the feelings that arose and did not explode, but reacted calmly. What they saw that night was the same situation replayed, but in the dream they got very angry.

In their waking hours after the dream, the thought that arose in the mind was to not be angry and the filter of the intellect worked and said, "I don't want to react in anger."

In the sleep state the filter is set aside, and so because the pattern of behaviour, i.e. to react angrily, was still carried within the unconscious, it was expressed in the dream, revealing to the person that anger was still there and that something needed to be done about it at a deeper level.

Patterns
within the Self

Our interactions with human beings during the day are usually functional and everything seems to be fine, yet in dreams I may see some image of a person which is a signal that there is something on another level that needs to be worked out within myself.

Often people speak to me about relationship problems, they say that one of the first signals they had that something was wrong was through a dream, but when they first had the dream, they were not able to accept or identify the real-life problem immediately. Weeks later, they realise that something was going on that they hadn't noticed at the time. Finally, when something drastic does happen, they wish they had picked up the signals earlier.

This process shows the connection of the patterns within the self, so that what is recorded deep within comes up to the surface later and needs to be faced and dealt with.

Dreams about the Future

—∞∞∞—

There is another type of sleeping dream, in which there is first a dream and then that situation actually happens. Sometimes it may be good, sometimes bad. I have heard many anecdotes of both. Typically what happens is that someone has a dream; they try to ignore it. They tell others and others tell them to ignore it, yet a little while later, whether days or weeks, that dream actually manifests itself in life as a reality.

Where did that image come from? What was being picked up at the moment of the dream? Is it possible that the soul not only has information within itself about the past, but also has recorded within itself some information about the future? Or is there some information in the ether 'out there' which I, the soul, am able to pick up?

In my experience, I have found that I am most likely to pick up such information when I am willing to let go of my identification with the body and the ego connected with it, and when I am also willing to let go of that filter of reason and logic in which everything has to 'make sense'. When all that has been put aside, it is then that I most easily pick up some information from 'outside myself' which then proves to be very much a reality.

This phenomenon has happened far too often, to far too many people, for us to just ignore it or say that it

is a fluke. Scientific practice
dictates that if an experiment
is repeated and yields the
same results many times,
I have to take the findings
seriously.

Inspirational
Dreams

As well as dreams which reveal the subconscious and dreams which foretell the future, there are also dreams that inspire. These dreams include those that we ourselves have, that uplift and guide us. They can also include dreams which other people have had, that give us inspiration and encouragement. And I would like to suggest that there is a third type of inspirational dream, a dimension where it is possible, within the so-called dream, to travel beyond presumed limits and barriers and experience reality which is at a distance from the location of the physical body.

A simple example of this, with which I am particularly familiar, is dreams in which people have been visited by yogis (people who practice Raja Yoga) with an inspiration or even with a very specific message, when there was no possibility of communication physically. From my own experience I would also place these dreams in the category of reality.

Déjà Vu

Déjà vu usually occurs when we are awake, yet it has many characteristics of a dream. My understanding of this phenomenon is based on my personal belief in rebirth, or reincarnation. For me the déjà vu experience is a powerful addition to the many factors that point to the reality that multiple human incarnations take place during the life of the eternal soul. What happens in déjà vu is that, for example, I may go somewhere that I have never visited before (in this lifetime)

and experience a memory or
a flashback that comes from
no conscious thought of my
own. This memory is so vivid
and personal, the experience
so real, that I am sure it is
not just something I have
seen in a photo or a film. This
phenomenon happens with
people as well as with places
or situations. I meet someone
whom I don't know and yet
I have a very deep feeling of
connection with this person.

Dreams about the future,
inspirational dreams and déjà

vu are all encompassed within this model of the soul. So what then is a dream and what is reality?

Reality, Dreams and Time

$\otimes\!\otimes\!\otimes$

I am reminded of a lovely description I heard of the distinction between a dream and reality, in terms of time. Every moment that has gone by has merged in the past and as such is already a dream. The only reality is now, this present moment. To be here in the present, this is my only reality. To cling to yesterday or yesteryear simply causes a burden and is a tremendous waste of energy. As well as seeing the sleeping dream as something to learn from, I can also treat all that is past as a great dream from which I am learning. This is a very interesting concept. To be stable in this awareness is something with which we can mentally experiment and work.

Every moment is a new birth; every second is an awakening, a new miracle. If we can enter each moment with a clean slate and not clutter it up with our projections from the past, then each moment will be fresh and unspoiled.

But it is no good trying to 'live in the present moment' to have that luminous, magical 'now', by denying the past. Because although we may think that we have re-fenced the 'now', if we have only managed to suppress the consequence or impact of those unpleasant and painful events from the past they will definitely come right back and spoil the 'present'.

We have to know the past for what it is and learn from it. We cannot change it, but

we can come to see that it
is sometimes giving us the
message that we had better
act and behave differently
both now and in the future.
We cannot ignore the past but
it is totally counterproductive
for us to get stuck in it or
obsessed by it so that it
overshadows every new
moment.

My experience has been that
when we don't learn the
lessons of the past, we hang
on to it and the past becomes
our present reality also.

However, when we are able to look at the past, and learn our lessons from it, then, like a dream which has served its purpose but whose time has now gone, it is possible to let go and move on into the reality of present.

About the Author

B.K Jayanti is a spiritual teacher and leader, a gifted meditator and an emissary for peace. She has a vision and experience that is truly global and deeply spiritual. Born in India of Sindhi parents, who migrated to England when she was eight years old, she is a blend of Eastern wisdom and western education and culture.

At the age of 19 she embarked on a journey of spiritual study and service with the Brahma Kumaris

World Spiritual University, and at the age of 21, decided to dedicate her life to this path. She has spent over 40 years in the company of some of the world's most remarkable yogis, gleaning much of their wisdom and insights. As a result, she herself is an extraordinary meditator and teacher and has developed a clarity and purity of mind that is exceptional. B.K. Jayanti is also a much sought-after speaker around the world.

Her natural wisdom and gentle, though powerful, personality have touched and inspired hundreds of thousands of people. She is the European Director of the Brahma Kumaris World Spiritual University and assists in co-ordinating the university's activities in more than 100 countries. She is also its main representative to the United Nations, Geneva.

About the Brahma Kumaris

The Brahma Kumaris is a network of organisations in over 100 countries, with its spiritual headquarters in Mt Abu, India. The University works at all levels of society for positive change. Acknowledging the intrinsic worth and goodness of the inner self, the University teaches a practical method of meditation that helps people to cultivate their inner strengths and values.

The University also offers courses and seminars in such topics as positive thinking, overcoming anger, stress relief and self-esteem, encouraging spirituality in daily life. This spiritual approach is also brought into healthcare, social work, education, prisons and other community settings.

The University's Academy in Mount Abu, Rajasthan, India, offers individuals from all backgrounds a variety of life-long learning opportunities to help them recognise their inherent qualities and abilities in order to make the most of their lives.

All courses and activities are offered free of charge.
Visit www.brahmakumaris.org for more information.

www.bkpublications.com

How and Where to Find Out More

SPIRITUAL HEADQUARTERS
PO Box No 2, Mount Abu 307501,
Rajasthan, India
Tel: (+91) 2974-238261 to 68
Fax: (+91) 2974-238883
E-mail: abu@bkivv.org

INTERNATIONAL CO-ORDINATING OFFICE & REGIONAL OFFICE FOR EUROPE AND THE MIDDLE EAST
Global Co-operation House,
65-69 Pound Lane,
London, NW10 2HH, UK
Tel: (+44) 20-8727-3350
Fax: (+44) 20-8727-3351
E-mail: london@brahmakumaris.org

REGIONAL OFFICES

AFRICA
Global Museum for a Better World,
Maua Close, off Parklands Road, Westlands
PO Box 123, Sarit Centre, Nairobi, Kenya
Tel: (+254) 20-374-3572
Fax: (+254) 20-374-3885
E-mail: nairobi@brahmakumaris.org

AUSTRALIA AND SOUTH EAST ASIA
78 Alt Street, Ashfield, Sydney, NSW 2131,
Australia
Tel: (+61) 2-9716-7066
Fax: (+61) 2-9716-7795
E-mail: ashfield@au.brahmakumaris.org

THE AMERICAS AND THE CARIBBEAN
Global Harmony House, 46 S.
Middle Neck Road,
Great Neck, NY 11021, USA
Tel: (+1) 516-773-0971
Fax: (+1) 516-773-0976
E-mail: newyork@brahmakumaris.org

RUSSIA, CIS AND THE BALTIC COUNTRIES
Brahma Kumaris World Spiritual University
2, Lobachika, Bldg. No. 2, Moscow - 107140,
RUSSIA
Tel: (+7) 499 2646276
Fax: (+7) 495-261-3224
www: brahmakumarisru.com
www: spiritual-development.ru
E-mail: moscow@brahmakumaris.org

www.bkpublications.com
E-mail: enquiries@bkpublications.com